STARLIGHT LIFE
N.C BRIGHTMAN

ISBN 978-1-66780-630-3

*"We are all of us stars,
and we deserve to twinkle"*

—Marilyn Monroe

TABLE OF CONTENTS

LIVE A STARLIGHT LIFE

To live a Starlight Life
is not to live without strife
There will be days of darkness and light,
like an inner day and night
Inside your heart and soul, there is a place to go
Where authenticity and love is always the goal
To the masking of self it says no.
It says "I love you unconditionally, I do not judge
When you slip up, I do not hold a grudge."
To live a Starlight Life is to look within
To be present and not treat the present as a sin
For it is human nature to project and look away
To live tomorrow, to live yesterday
and forget about today
To live a Starlight Life, is to live another way
To breathe, to centre yourself in the here and now
To find a space within, that knows the inner you
and takes your soul to a happy place
It whispers sweet words, with love and grace
I love you, I care and I say this now my friend
Your greatest power is to be you
and I will guide you, until the very end

LOVE ALL OF YOU

Love all of you like no one else can
Don't wait for a woman, don't wait for a man
Love all of you, every single part
When you do, wonder fills your heart
Forgive yourself when you stumble and fall
Stand strong in yourself and your spirit feels tall
Love yourself, for you are with you at all time
In presence, in thoughts and in every way
Your choices for you should feel divine
and bring love and joy to your day
Love yourself, so you can live a happy life.
Wait not for a partner, husband or wife
Look in the mirror, and say "I love you."
Put your hand on your heart and say it again
Live a life that reflects your desires for you
and you will have less inner pain
Love all of you and when you speak of yourself
Speak as you would to your best friend
Take your needs and your dreams off the dusty shelf
Then see them through to the finished end
Love all of you, to do so is not selfish or weak
It is a selfless act so to speak.
For we can spread this love outwards and above
All over the world, like butter over bread
There is so much good to be said
Love all of you
so others can too

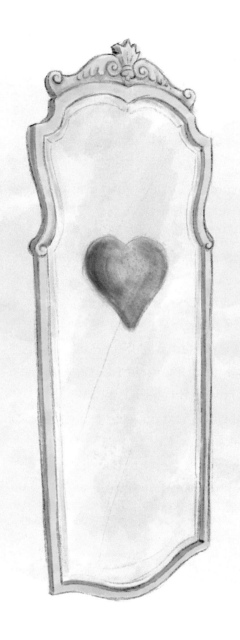

SWEET SILENCE

There's beauty in music and sound
But in silence, true beauty can be found.
When in silence, I can look without the need to label
When in silence, my inner world suddenly seems more stable
Silence comes if you allow it, it does not haste
Silence is sweet, like a strawberry's sweet taste
Silence has something that the mind cannot comprehend
 Yet the soul understands it well
It has no beginning and no end
It is an eternal everlasting spell
Yet inner silence cannot arrive if you do not allow it in
Like clouds blocking out the sun's light,
the darkness will sometimes win.
 Our inner light is beautiful and so bright
With silence and inner focus, we can see it shine
Just be present now in this moment of time
It is in silence that we hear our soul's inner sound
It is strawberry sweet and all around
It forgives you if you forget to acknowledge it,
and illuminates your world, if you allow even a little bit

NEVER TOO LATE TO START AGAIN

Life can be full of hurt and pain
But it's never too late to start again
Like the caterpillar that becomes a butterfly.
Like dust clouds in the galaxy, that turn into the stars of
the sky
We may say we are too young, or too old
But life is better lived when we are bold
There is so much that we could gain
from living for ourselves, and being who we are meant to be
You have so much to give, don't you see ?
It's never too late to start again
Let go of regret that has built up within
Like the clouds shed the rain
May you follow your path and grow like a flower
It's never too late to start again, may you start in this hour

GAZING AT THE STARS

I don't know the way to heaven's gate
I can't see you anymore
Ever since you met your fate
and slipped through heaven's door
So I'm gazing at the stars
to imagine where you are
The world above the eye,
beyond earth's sky
Has a presence of mystery
I wonder where you could be
I can't find you
Like a child playing hide and seek
I can't hear your voice
replying to me when I speak
I don't have a choice
I can't see you here
So I'm gazing at the stars
I feel you all around
I can't find you here
but something is still found
Heaven speaks in the star diamond sky
I know your spirit came to fly
I feel you in the night sky's beating heart
Here we are together, even though we are apart
I'm gazing at the stars
The wonder of the world above
makes up for all that I lack.

In the void that was made when you were gone
For in the peace and serenity of the night, I feel like I have
you back.
I feel your whisper in the wind saying "My dear child, you
are not alone."
I'm gazing at the stars, and I feel like you are home

UNSEEN BLANKET

I heard your prayer today
asking for another way
You don't see me
You sense me around
Like the roots of a tree,
deep in the ground.
I nurture you, I comfort you
when you are lost on what to do
Sometimes you may feel me nearby
When you need help, or when you're calm
Like a soft, soothing balm
Do not fear me,
I only wish to love you
Do not fear me,
I only wish to guide you
When you are lost in this maze of your life
When hope seems far from your reach
Like the tide going out on the beach
I only want what is best for you
I will guide you to the tide of hope
So you can find the shells of guidance
There is no need for fear and avoidance
I am here for you
Talk to me if you need me
I am only a thought away
As close as I can be
I hear you when you pray

I am your unseen blanket

I was here for you before you came to earth

I stayed here after your birth

In this life I will always be by your side

I am your one true guide

ONE LOVE

We only have one love forever
To leave, I can never
Sometimes it can be hard
I can feel sad and jarred
I always feel what they feel
It can make me reel
Sometimes I want to break up
Since I can't go,
I have to kiss and make up
I'm with them all the time
Even when I wish that I was not
Sometimes it's like a mine
with no gold left, long forgot
But when I remember
to love and be patient
It's like Christmas in December
I can open the gift of love and joy
I feel like a shiny new toy.
when I'm at one with my one love
This is a force from above
and who is it, you may ask.
This person, loving them can be a hard task,
but a joy if done well
Who is there in this forever spell ?
That person is me

So you see
If you treasure your one love
It becomes easier to treasure others too
For it is easier to love another
If you can look within and say "I love you."

COURAGE'S FLAMES

On a path we want to take, but fear keeps us still
On a seesaw between refusal and will
There seems to be flames in the way
There have been flames in my path before
Burning in front of me as bright as day
I didn't know what to do any more
I waited and waited, hoping they'd become easier to
get through
Waiting was all that I seemed to do
The flames that burned, they didn't seem to change
But maybe I did, just a little bit
Something tiny inside me lit
The desire for change, stronger than the fear of the fire
So I leapt fearfully through the pyre
When I leaped, I came to realise
That the flames that seemed to reach the skies
Burned deeper within me, than without
After the leap, the flames changed from flames of doubt
To flames of courage and power
They no longer razed me alive, but gave me life
Like a wonderful, invigorating shower
The flames of courage built me up, so I could one day
leap again
For to leap into uncertainty, even when you are afraid
That's how you know the flames of courage have been made

CANDLE OF MORTALITY

Life is like a candle flame,
it could flicker out anytime
Life is far from tame,
it's like a monkey on a vine
Life is like a tide,
it's a crazy fast ride
Like a sunset,
it can go down too fast
You have no way to truly bet,
which moment will be your last
That's what makes it sad,
but it also makes us glad
For if we lived this life forever more
There would be less to live for
But sometimes we forget,
and are caught up in a net
Of making ends meet,
and rushing from our seat
Instead of smelling the morning dew,
and letting presence come through
Look at nature, and you'll see
how living can be
Listen to the birdsong
of unity, so strong
Never caring if the tune is wrong,
and just singing for the love

Can we live like the bird,
and let our love be heard ?
For we are like the candle's mortality flame
Not knowing how long we have, before we wane
Let us learn to live again, rather than just survive
I believe that we can learn to live
By remembering that we are beautiful beings of life
Like the sunset, the birds and the sea
Like the candle of mortality
You are a beautiful life, as beautiful as can be

SONG OF LIFE

My life is like a song
Every day is like a tune
to which I sing along
Like an air balloon,
every second floats along
Tomorrow becomes today,
yesterday melts away
My song is not all my own
My tune has come and grown
from the songs of others, that have gone before .
Their name still sings today,
at the present's door
Through memories and words of hope
Even though their body's life script is no more.
My song and the song of others
will never truly go away.
So long as people sing along,
and keep the lyrics strong

LIVING FOR ME

Who are you going to be ?
What kind of life do you want to see ?
These are the questions you want to ask yourself.
Am I living this life for me,
or am I sleepwalking through the dreams of someone else ?
We often tell ourselves that we aren't enough
But those words feel like liquorice, dark and sticky stuff
Are you living a life that belongs to the wishes of you ?
Or are you like a genie, making the wishes of another come true?
We are only human, and we want to make everyone happy
But sometimes we need to have clarity
Go within, be still and ask yourself.
Am I living for me ?
Am I being who I want to be ?
Or am I wearing someone else's glasses, unable to see ?
Nobody else can be you, better than you can
Nobody else can be the same woman, or man
No one else can be this version of you
I can't make you decide if you want to see this through
I can't make you decide to be yourself or not.
Maybe you don't want to hurt anybody.
But that will happen anyway.
Because the hurt inside your soul,
is the longest hurt to stay.
You can't please everyone around you.
But you can ask yourself
Am I living for me ?
Am I being who I want to be ?

DANCING WITH DOUBT

When you have a challenge in life
A musical dance will start
A dance of doubt, fast beating of the heart
With each beat, you want to retreat
It's a dance between fear and love.
Half of you wants to stay
The other half wants to run away
In the dance, the dance with doubt
Love and fear, both come out
Heart beats with passion and fear
Will the dance continue,
or is the end near ?
Sometimes we leave, and sometimes we stay
It can go either way
In this dance with doubt
It doesn't seem to get easier,
but we can get braver
One beat of love can beat louder
We can dance prouder,
in the dance with doubt

LIVE BEFORE I DIE

To live before I die,
is to let my hopes fly
My dreams can only survive,
if I move and let them drive.
To live before I die
I laugh and I cry
To live and feel
makes your life real
I can only do this, when I allow myself to simply be
and live my life as me.
So by enjoying the little things,
like sunny days and water springs
By allowing myself to live in the now,
and knowing that somehow
If I am to live before I die
I can and must try
To be nobody but me
and allow myself to see
The entrancing beauty of this day,
as I walk my journey's way
Work towards your goal's gate,
but enjoy the path you lead
Spend more on love than hate,
and take heed
I wish to live before I die
and sometimes I fail, but I try

Each day is better to live,
if you feel blessed and give
To live before you die
is to love, simply be, and try

SEEING RAINBOWS

Sometimes they see rainbows
Sometimes they see black
Either way they look at me,
without turning back
When they look at me, their thoughts will be
on a different path to before
Very soon I'll have moved on,
and my presence is no more
One minute I can be there,
in a swirl of skirts I'm gone
I leave behind a trail,
as bright as the sun
It shines in people's hearts
with joy, grace, and fun
I leave messages wherever I go
To tell people things and show
Who I may be, and what I do.
If you need me, I come to you
I do not read letters, nor do I answer calls
In time of need, I'll answer your wish or prayer
When the sun shines, or the snow falls
I'll be at your door
Waiting to help you heal your sorrows,
and smile once more

DEAD I AM NOT

I am many things now, but dead I am not
I am in a land, that those on earth have forgot
I shed my body, I left it behind
I am in a place of spirit and mind
I am invisible to the eye, but you may sense me around
In the gentle touch to your cheek
The penny you find on the ground
Sometimes you may hear me speak
in my favourite song, that the radio decides to play
At other times, you may dream of me
Know that I am here, I have not gone away
I am in another place of living, where physical pain is
no more
I am not dead, I am simply behind another door
Know that I am happy, and that I am here for you
I will hold you tight, when you feel blue
Live your life as best as you can, and know this
That when your time comes to join me,
I'll greet you with a kiss

NO LANGUAGE FOR LOVE

Whatever tongue I speak
Whatever language I say
There's a community streak,
that touches all today
There's no language for an embrace
No language for a smile on someone's face
Dancing has no word
No communication unheard
There's no language for love
For things we don't say
that we decide to do
There's no language for love,
it is a communication for all
A place where language barriers fall
The language of one
that is life, that is love

MOTIVATION

I have motivation
for my life's creation
To wake up and sleep
To swim shallow or deep
I have motivation
and imagination
To create the life I choose
Whether I win or lose
I may stumble and fall
But I stand so tall
I am feeling strong
I have motivation
in who I am and what I do
My imagination
it runs through and through
Whether I'm following a path along
To something I choose to complete
There's nowhere better to belong
Than where I walk with my own two feet
May your motivation guide and inspire you
Keep flowing along
If you follow your heart and intuition
You can flow along with your ambition
May motivation keep you walking along
In the direction that you belong

For there's no better path for you
than the one you walk consciously
May you find it and walk through
with motivation and clarity

A LITTLE BIT UNIQUE

There's a pattern in the snowflakes falling from the sky
A little bit of unique falling on by
There's comfort in the raindrops, falling on my window
As I sit by the fireplace with nowhere to go
There's a little bit of unique in nature, and us all
From the daisies in the springtime, to the leaves in the fall
This is what makes us the soul, that we are meant to be
It's in all that we do, and the perception that we see
There's curiosity in the sand grains underneath my toe
As I leave the seaside, they don't care where I go
A little bit of unique is in everything
from the breeze in the air, and the birds that sing
We think that so many things are the same
and from a distance that seems true
But look closer, and the differences appear again
The same applies to you
There's a little bit of unique in us all
It's beautiful and magical
So please don't change the unique in you
In the unique, there is love

LITTLE THINGS

Little things have so much to give,
that brighten the way we live
A sunset on a summer's night
clears the mind, and makes the soul bright
A cup of tea on a Monday morning,
brings gladness to the day dawning
A kiss goodnight before you go to bed,
invites peace as you rest your head
The walk with your dog along the beach,
brings serenity when it seemed out of reach
Like the butterfly that finds the flower,
the little things have the power
To steer your soul on its merry way,
when you invite them in today

SAFE DAYDREAM

Sometimes when I dream by day
It's for more than fantasy play
It is more than just dragons and magic spells.
More than coins in wishing wells
I dream of a safe daydream
A world where the very threat of the earth,
is not in frequent jeopardy
To have to access this land, through a safe daydream
is normalised, but it is a tragedy
As long as the place that keeps us alive today,
is being destroyed in almost every way
Even as you sit here and read,
the mind will sometimes plant a seed
That grows to a safe daydream
Of a world where we have balance, and no longer destroy
A world with a harmonious envoy
If I could go within, and project my safe daydream
Around the world, until peace become mainstream
I would do it now in love and light
So the world can become jovial and bright

LOST THE CHILD

When we were young, we longed to play
We found the fun in every day
We made sandcastles on the beach
Joy and rapture were easy to reach
Then little by little, we lost the child
We became less merry, we became less wild
We became too busy to laugh and play
We simply focused on surviving each day
Our inner voice and faith had little room,
to inspire wisdoms to grow and bloom
Our rational minds had run the race
Setting life at a fast and worrying pace
Until one day, when it became too much
We had all but lost life's loving touch
We had lost the child, that made us smile
It had left our sides for a while
Not gone but lost, waiting to be found
Longing to bring fun back into life's playground
So we reached within, and took our inner child by the hand
Then once again, life seemed a little more grand
We took the time to run around and play,
adding a few treats into our day
Taking up hobbies, playing sports in the sun
Suddenly life seems much more fun.
Of course, there are things we all need to do,
but taking time for fun makes us feel less blue

SNOW DAY

There's no day like a snow day
When snowflakes fall my way
The world looks like a Christmas card
The grounds are white, and ponds are hard
Children building snowmen, searching for the eyes and nose
Snowflakes falling on my clothes
There's no day like a snow day, the world is a fairy-tale land
Couples walk down the street, hand in hand
Snow angels cover the ground
I go ice skating round and round,
trying to stay upon my feet
Days like this are such a treat
There's no day like a snow day
When I go downhill on my bright red sleigh,
I feel like Santa Claus, happy and jolly
On my door is a wreath with holly
When I am home, I have hot chocolate by the fire
Snow days are my winter's desire,
especially when Christmas comes around
I love it when snow covers the ground
There's no day like a snow day

BLACKBERRY DREAMS

We all have dreams before us
We all have obstacles to climb
Like the blackberries to pick in autumn time,
there's an obstacle blocking our way
We get nettled and pricked, and cry in dismay
When we reach for the berries, and dreams out there
The brambles get tangled and caught in our hair
The way to our dreams, it seems so far
Those blackberry dreams, we long for them so
But to make them reality, can be painful and slow
We may want to stop, when we get nettled and stung
We can quit, or we can keep our faith sweet and strong
For like the berry's journey, from flower to fruit
Some things take time to grow
So when you want to follow a dream,
or make blackberry pie
Remember blackberry dreams,
and don't be afraid to try

A LIFE WITHOUT RAIN

I used to long for a life without rain
At a time of little joy, and much pain
There were too many clouds to see the light
I only wanted a sky that is clear and bright
But then I remembered the power of the sun,
after a day of rain, when the skies were glum
Then I smiled, and knew that I was right
To say that we cannot have no darkness, and just light
We cannot have a life without rain
As we would not see compassion, in times of pain
We would not appreciate the moments we have had
We would not feel so glad
There would be no rainbows after a stormy day
May we be united in love and light
Since we cannot make all darkness go away
But bless the darkness at day, and night
And pray that it brings out our lights
Pray that it makes us love, and be kind
Since we cannot live without rain

BREATH BECOMES LIFE

When life becomes hard, and the world feels cold
When joy feels hard to hold
Sit down dear friend and breathe
Breathe, and feel your breath keeping you here
Like a constant step to retrieve
the next moment, to hold dear
Breath becomes life, when you hold it close
Breath becomes life, when you feel it
rushing in through your nose,
and outwards again
Breath becomes life, rushing around the pain
You have a breath inside, that loves you
A breath inside, that works for you
A breath that says "You can do it."
A breath that says "I am here."
A breath that brings in new energy,
whilst releasing the old
A breath to lessen fear
A message to say "Look within, for the answers lie inside."
Like breath in your lungs,
and love in your heart.
Wisdom and answers are your truth,
from which you can never be apart
You may forget to feel your breath
You may shut away your heart
But that does not change the truth
That you are a living, loving work of art

So breathe, and feel your breath
Feel love beat through your heart
Then you can trust your inner guide
that is within, with love inside

REACH TO ME

World's beyond the eyes,
possibility with surprise
New ideas, a new change for all.
Let the old ways fall
Let us choose to heal, rather than self-destruct
Let go of what does not serve you
Let it go, into the blue.
I know that peace and dreams
seem far over the rainbow
Change is closer than it seems
just so you know
New ideas are here
They say reach to me,
bring me near
So a new world can be
We only have today,
to make change come our way
Reach to me, don't turn away
Let a new world come,
so change can arrive
We've only just begun
Let us stay alive
Reach to me
May we make a future, that we can see

ANGEL EVERY DAY

I want to be an angel every day
That's something I just can't be
I want to be of only light
No darkness within me
It makes me sad,
and far from glad
When I try and fail, to be this way
I can't be an angel every day
Sometimes I feel like
I'm on a big, long hike
Where I'm trying to help every other soul,
but I'm leaving myself behind
We must make self-care our goal,
as sometimes we can be
An angel that cannot see
that compassion for self, is what we need
On a chain that is the final bead,
to hold the others in place
All we need is space
to make mistakes, and learn
Self-love is something we have,
not something we earn
I can't be an angel every day,
but I can love myself anyway

MUSIC OF ME

All of the human race has a song inside
To which they dance, or step aside
Some people stand up and dance, for most of their time here
While some turn away from the song, until they
both disappear
The music within us, is a different song to all
We all have a different musical purpose, to dance to at
life's ball
Each purpose sounds different to all, like drums and a flute
Whatever the sound, the song within wishes to grow
I could let the music of me become mute,
or I could finish the show
The music of me sings in my chi
It plays again and again, willing me to my feet
Through each note it asks
"Do you want this song to come to be ?"
The music of me wants me to meet
a life, where I listen to the song inside
The music wishes for us to no longer hide
It dreams of a ball of life, where everyone decides to dance
I hear you music, I hear you loud and clear
To the dance floor, I skip and prance
So that my song can outwardly appear
Follow the music of your dreams, for your song is your own
You have a piece within, that belongs to you alone

THE PRISON OF CAN'T

I trapped myself in the prison of can't
When doubt and tarry followed me along
The prison of can't, it held me
When I gave in to the doubts, and felt anything but strong
Can't is a way, that the mind decides to say
I have not yet done this, so I cannot see
How this outcome can ever come to be
If you are in the prison of can't, don't judge yourself
too harshly
For within you lies the key, the key to set yourself free
The key to freedom is an open mind
To know that there are many possibilities to find
If the prison of can't held more of mankind
Then I may not have the way
To write you this poem today
No computer or electricity
Would have come to be
This, and many other things within your sight
Would not have been made, for your delight
The prison of can't, it follows us all throughout our life
But it is up to us to decide.
Whether to walk away, or go inside.
So we can choose whether to stay in the prison of can't
Or free ourselves for the freedom of can
I know that you have the power to set yourself free
There is so much that you can do, so much you could be
But I do not have the key to let you out of jail

The only one who can give you bail
Can be found when you look in a mirror
I know that you can deliver for yourself, and set yourself free
But that outcome will only come to be
If you believe too
If the prison of can't is holding you in
The freedom of can, will break you through

I AM A KALEIDOSCOPE

I am a kaleidoscope of many a sort
Created from what I've learned and taught
I'm shaken up and patterns fly
Pictures say hello, and goodbye
There's circles of the sad
Stars of the glad.
Hearts of the love
Squares of the mad
Like being held by a glove
Life shakes me about
There's shapes of doubt
Shapes of belief
I am a kaleidoscope, it's what I'm about
Moments come and go like a thief
A world of kaleidoscopes is what we are
We can be shaken so far,
make pictures as we go
Like the skies above and the ground below
May we shake as our wonderful selves,
but also shake as one

CAN YOU AND ME, FORGIVE ME ?

Can you forgive me for what I did to you ?
The guilt is eating me alive, and making me blue
I saw a side of myself that I did not know was there
Like dandruff underneath my hair,
it came out and made a mess
Now I find it hard to forgive me
It causes me so much pain and stress.
I can't see straight any more
Forgiveness is the clarity needed for
a clearer, and uplifted sense of self
I left that part of me upon a shelf,
that I cannot seem to reach
A lesson I need to learn, and teach
Can you and me, forgive me ?
For what I did to you,
and what I did to myself, out of guilt
I wronged you, that much is true.
I know that from the pain I felt
coming from you, and then from me
Can you and me forgive me ?
It's a place that feels hard to reach
But a place we one day need to be
I'm sorry for everything I did to you
I ask for forgiveness, from a place that is true
One day, I hope that we can be,
in a place where you and me, can forgive me
So we can once more, feel free

I CAN'T BE PERFECT

Gone a day
where my inner routine fell underway
Spoiled my style of hair
I didn't feel all there
I lost my charm and my smile
Not a good style
But how can I hold on always,
when I am always feeling new ?
I can't be perfect,
but I can be real
I am still worth it,
because I am trying to make a better deal
of myself.
I sometimes need help,
if I fall downwards in motion
But it's not the ocean,
it's just a mighty raindrop
It can be brought to a stop,
when I just accept myself
You're beautiful, don't you see ?

A MOMENT OF GRACE

Life is like a dance,
where we all twist and prance
A dance through which we stumble and fall
but we rise again, and stand tall.
Life is like a dance,
it's slow yet fast
Each step comes, before we can savour the last
Life is like a dance,
it's tiring and dizzy
We dance too fast and get in a tizzy
Our dance needs a moment of grace
So we can feel each step, and enjoy the space
to breathe, to move, to laugh and love
To enjoy the lights from high above,
of the sun, the stars, and the moon
Such wonders we see so soon
That we look upon, without seeing
A dance without being,
is a dance without life
A moment of grace, then another and another
Can help us embrace this dance,
like a child embraces their mother

LIFE OF CLAY

My mind and bones are made of clay
My existence changes every day
Even when everything seems the same,
no same day will ever come again
My life is a book,
with new events wherever you look
My mind is made of clay
It changes shape every day
To the books of life
and the minds of clay
I know that you may
be bored, and feel alone
Remember that clay can change in shape,
and stories can change in tone
The animals of books and clay
They know that this is the way
That stories and clay change again, and again
We all live a life of stories and clay
Let us shape and write
our day and night
In this moment of beauty
So we can simply be, again

UGLY TO YOU

Spiders with many legs and eyes
That crawl, and trap the flies
We run far as a slipper flies at us,
and hear people scream, as they flee
I know you hate the sight of me,
I'm scared of you too
This is my life, I mean no harm
Yet I'm ugly to you
I know you love the butterflies,
that flutter gracefully through the skies
The ladybirds too, with their dainty spots of black
To me though, you turn your back
I make a web of soft silky art
It takes an hour for me to make
Yet in seconds, you take it apart
Then I have to start again, for survivals sake.
You think I'm ugly, that's sad to me
I know I am something that you don't like to see
I may not have artists wings
But I have beautiful things
in my appearance too
This is what you can do
If you see me inside,
please don't run and hide
Don't throw a slipper to kill me.
just because I'm ugly

Catch me and free me,
so that I may live
I'm sorry that I scared you
I hope that you forgive
I know I'm ugly to you
But I want to live, and be loved too

NOBODY COMPARES TO YOU

There's me and you
There's you and me
There's red and blue
There's a flower and a tree
Comparisons fill the world,
but nobody compares to you
The world might want to change around
Wondering who to be, and what to do
I'll keep your feet on the ground,
as nobody compares to you
Nobody compares to you, we are all unique
We have different lives and dreams to seek
Like colours of the rainbow, raindrops in the sky
Like dandelion clocks, the ways that they fly
We are all as one, yet we are numbers too
For being the same would never do
Our hearts may beat as one,
but our blood runs different ways
Nobody compares to you

AUTUMN LANE

When the old falls away,
leaving the sky
When what once was, goes on by
When everything changes
That's when I'm walking down autumn lane
When things change again, then again
Hello autumn lane, we meet once more
What once was here,
has fallen to past's floor
After becoming a beautiful, colourful memory
After a long holiday,
where I once rested in summer's bay
I've now found autumn lane,
to remind me that things will never stay the same
I might miss you summer's bay,
but I can't stay here every day
Autumn lane is here again,
to tell me and show me, that nothing stays the same

WHAT IS WRITING ?

I have a world within my mind,
only imagination can find
A story untrue to the real world,
that is real in my head
I am God to this land
The fates of all are in my hand
Or I am the curious watcher looking on,
at new worlds come and gone
Writing new friends to life one day
Then holding them in your heart and soul
Reading a book, is watching events and worlds, come to play
When tragedy strikes, it leaves a hole
Writing and reading bring people together
So stories can join minds and hearts forever

TOO LATE

It's too late to make a better yesterday,
for the present is gone there
The time is now today
I know it is unfair,
to think of everything you could have done
It's too late to make more fun,
of the time that has come, and had to go
Like every moment, they have their sunshine
Then they became a time of past,
that can only be reached by memory
We keep those times alive in you and me,
through photos and our mind
Reaching that time physically, is something we cannot find
It's too late to paint a new picture in this gallery.
Even though I wished for better for you, and for me
New canvases of blank white,
are now there for paint, and present light
We cannot rewrite what has already been wrote,
but we can write and paint a new day
So that we can have less regrets in the present's note
The present will always be here to stay.
So let us paint the best picture, and write the best story
It's too late to rewrite those past times, now distant and gone
But we can write, and paint a present of glory

AWAKE THROUGH
THE THUNDERSTORMS

Are we awake through a thunderstorm ?

When lightning and sound jolts you awake

Into awake you are reborn

Returning to sleep is a hard road to take

For there are storms outside

With purple flashes and rumblings above

There are storms inside

In the name of fear and love

Thoughts keep flashing through the mind

They feel loud, and all-consuming to me

Anxieties are easy to find

Like lightning, so easy to see

Can I sleep through the storm tonight ?

Rather than staying wide awake

There's a light within so bright

A calm path I could take

If I can only breathe and let go

Make mindfulness the star of the show

Let thoughts pass on through

Without judgment of what the thoughts say, and do

Then the storms won't keep me awake

I can let lightning thoughts flash by

Let the rumblings just be noise

The storm in the sky

I can sleep through it tonight
You can sleep tonight
I've been awake through the storms before
But now I go through slumber's door

MOVIE MIND

I have a movie mind, that skips and changes all the time
Sometimes the story is just fine,
at other times it is a mess
Believing the movie, can cause such stress,
when you don't think that the script is right
Sometimes the movie can run late into the night,
when you want to stop and sleep
Sometimes you feel like you're in too deep
This plot of twists, unfolding into something new
Like a seed, anxiety just grew and grew
This fast and wild movie mind,
is not always sweet and kind
It can send you spinning into a downward spiral, pulling
you under
This movie is in such a blunder
So watch it, like you would watch a TV
To the movie, be a neutral party
You can watch it in curiosity, without letting panic fly
Worry not about the content
Let it spin down, like a penny into a vortex box
Watch it like you would that penny, that penny so well spent
Put on your comfy socks
and watch your thoughts, with your mind's eye
You and I have a movie mind
It won't always be quiet

So watch what it will find
I am not my movie mind
I am the curious watcher, watching what is inside

HERO SLEEPS

Today the hero sleeps,
they're tired from saving everyone
The hero and I are one
We are tired from running about,
saving the world from pain and doubt
Even a hero needs to rest,
and free the worries within from their chest
I can't be everything to everyone,
but my journey hasn't ended, it has just begun
I am my own hero today,
using my power in the best way
By nourishing my soul, and caring for me
A day off duty
But I'll be there, I'll be back again
To save the world from pain
When I have recharged myself once more
Heroes of the world, take time to sleep
Take time out, before demands become too steep
Step aside, before you get stuck in the mud
For running on an empty cup, will do you no good

LIGHT OF THE MOON

By the light of the moon, I wander
A pearly globe shining above
A world spotlight, I walk under
A light of mystery and love
This is the light that makes waves move
The light to make a wolf howl
A beautiful sky treasure, so shiny and smooth
It makes my primitive spirit prowl
I could look at you all night, sweet light of the moon
You move as I walk, like a luminescent balloon
Man walked upon you, in nineteen sixty nine
They jumped, and moved on your dancing light
Your light is of such wonder
That they dreamt of you day and night,
until they landed upon your twirling glow
Filmed it for all the world, a wonderful show
I may never dance upon your wonderful light
But I can see you glowing in the sky at night
Light of the moon, you inspire me so
You are above me, or are you below ?
Either way, my eyes admire you so

WONDERLAND

The sky is azure blue
Beauty that's so true
The sun is like a glowing buttercup
The sight of it lifts you up
By nightfall, I see stars in my eyes
As I look in the skies
I'm in a wonderland
That's taking me by the hand
The beauty of nature
coming from our Creator
Universe, stars, man and sky
It's a beauty that can make me cry
And I don't know why
But when I see the stars
It's like music to my eyes
If stars were a sound, they'd be guitars
The universe plays to my eyes as I look up
Wonder filling the universal cup
I could stay here forever in this wonderland
But I must rise from the outdoors tonight
and sleep inside
Wonderland is beautiful and bright
Why is there a divide
between us all ?
Can we just let it fall ?
Let it fall
Let it fall
So we can all be in wonderland

OCEAN HEART

My heart is like an ocean
Light sends it into motion
Like the moon above the earth,
it makes my heart rebirth
My heart is like an ocean,
it's full of depth, and swimming with life inside
The water lapping, is like my heart beat sound.
Beauty makes my heart glide
Heartache makes it fall to the ground
My heart is like an ocean,
it loves the island paradise sun
When I am in the waves, I feel like we are one
My heart is like an ocean
Longing for joy and beauty is a devotion.
May we take care of the world, and take care of our heart
So greed and misgivings don't tear us apart

AWAKE AGAIN

I was asleep in a bed of lies, and pain
Now I am up and awake again
There was a bed of darkness, pulling me to sleep
No faith, afraid to take a leap.
Now I am sleeping in this bed no more
Staved off the shadow wanting me to sleep
It didn't want me to move, it was afraid
A bed of fear and lies was made
Now my alarm has rung inside,
from this dark and heavy sleep
I no longer reside
I am awake again, faith helped me leap
I am awake, and wonder helped me up
Now drinking from the glass half full cup
To those asleep today
I think of you and pray
that you too, will be awake again

WHAT IS BRAVE ?

We think of a knight on a white horse,
when we think of Brave
But what course of reality can you say,
will make Brave come your way ?
We all have a spark of Brave,
of which we all crave
But how do we make it grow ?
How can Brave come to the show ?
Brave is not only in the big, and the strong
In every heart, Brave can belong
Brave comes without much thought,
but with risk too
Brave cannot be bought
Brave comes out of the blue,
from a will to make things right
A little spark of Just, shining bright
Pushing you forth into the unknown
The way for Brave to be grown,
is by holding tight,
and doing what you feel is right
Acting in spite of fear
Brave holds your spark dear
If you want a life, that is lived with growth and risk
Not knowing what concoction it may whisk,
but wishing to grow and find your feet
Hold Brave's hand, while you see what wonder and crazy
you meet

PRESENCE OF YOU

I miss the presence of you
I miss the wonder of you
The way you felt in a warm embrace
The sunshine smile upon your face
I know that you're around
I can sense you near
But your presence is not found
I wish I could see you here
 I miss the times that we had
I should be so glad
That what we have is something
That makes me miss you to this day
Like the cold winter grass misses the flowers, and warmth
of spring
Remembering you and sensing you around
Warms the cold void left inside
But it doesn't take it all away
I know your essence lives on
I know that you have not truly gone
But I still miss the presence of you
There is so much that I would love to do
If I had just one more day
One more chance, to have the presence of you
The part of me, that is like the cold grass of winter time
Would blossom into the joys of spring
If one more day of the presence of you, could be mine

STAR DREAMERS

What if stars are nature's dreamers ?
That one day decided, that they could become a light
A light for all of space to see,
that became visible to the worlds at night
The dreamers became a galaxy
Then the galaxies multiplied
The stars are like our dreams
They warm our world as they shine,
within our soul, like beams
For those of you, who are trying to follow your dreams
If the stars could speak, they'd say "You can do it."
Because before they became a star,
they had to come far
Before becoming the beautiful plasma that they are today
So to the dreamers of the world, I send love your way
Shine your light, and follow your dream
So another dreamer's light can be seen
Rub your best elements together, to make your dreams
come true
For there is a star within you

A THOUSAND STEPS

I look up at the staircase of my vision of me
So much that I want to be
I want it today, I want it now
I can't see how it will become a reality
I must remember my patience and sanity
Remember these words, remember this truth for all
Life is made of a thousand steps, a thousand steps or more
A thousand more for every door
Every milestone from start to end
Every dream, every turn and bend
You can't jump a whole staircase to the top
If you tried, you'd fall and drop
You'd crash downwards again,
with a feeling of emotional pain
Life is made of mountains high,
with destinations in the sky
You cannot jump up to the peak.
You'd fall down in a painful streak
Wonder and rooms are at the top of each
They are not so far out of reach
Take each step, one at a time
Be gentle on the journey's climb
Everyone goes at their own pace
Life is a climb, it's not a race
There are a thousand steps in life, a thousand steps and more
Step forwards my friend, till you reach journey's door

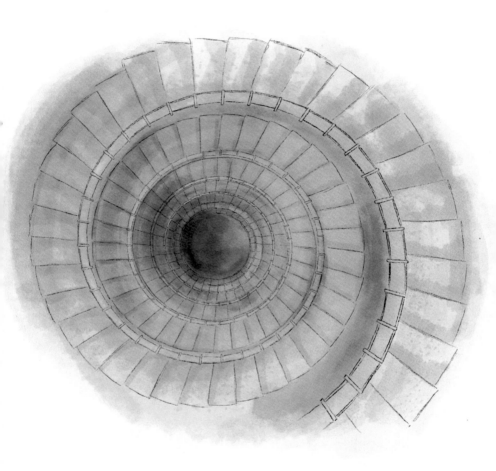

DO IT ANYWAY

There's a voice inside,
that wants me to run and hide
Happy to keep me in one place
No new adventures, no new face
The voice it tries to stop me, it says
"You can't finish the path to your dream."
I'll do it anyway
"Just you wait another day."
I'll go anyway
"Keep inside what you want to say."
I'll say it anyway
"Don't you dare to hope, or to dream."
I'll dream it anyway
And if I listened to you
I wouldn't finish what I want to do
You tell me that I'm not enough,
in one way or another
You'd stop me flying high above,
and embracing uncertainty like a brother
I let you hold me back before
Now I shake your hand in a parting way,
and walk through another door

COCOON

I'm in my metaphorical cocoon
I'm about to rise and bloom
I'm going to show the world what I'm made of
I'm about to fly, like a free and happy dove
I want to break open this last piece of shell
A part of me wonders, will it go well ?
How will things be, when I make this next change ?
Is it worth the risk, to open to this next life stage ?
I have a dream inside
I've been placing the pieces together
There's a cocoon in which I hide
Break out, and things could change forever
I'm excited, but I'm afraid
Of the changes that could be made
Will my plan bring a celebration in my life ?
Will it cause a strife ?
Will it be worth the time and sacrifice ?
This cocoon is suffocating, but it's safe inside
A part of me still wants to hide
For while there's a piece of me
that is crying, and longing to break free
Another piece of me, wants to stay within the dark
It shivers, it's afraid that this spark
May cause a burn, not a wonderful safe bonfire
It fears the destruction, that may come of this desire
The rest of me wants to tear this cocoon apart
Longing to reach the finish, after a run from the start

Cocoon, I want to break away,
to see what life sparks come my way
May this caterpillar become a butterfly,
and soar to the sky

YOU DID IT

When you feel low,
and you don't know where to go
Remember the time
when you did it
When you walked the line,
and made it across
When you won after a loss.
When you swam through the murky water
Can you feel what victory brought you ?
You did it
Despite the sceptics, and the doubt
Even what you wanted out,
you did it
You dared to dream,
though an end could not be seen
You did it,
and I'm proud of you
Don't you know all that you can do ?
Don't you know ?
All that you came through
You are the person you are today,
because you went all the way
You dared to dream and pray
You dared to believe that someday,
you'd hold hands with your dream
My friend, I believe in you

Look back on where you've been,
and how far you've come
It was a race to the rising sun
A race that you won
I know that you can win again
I know that despite the storms, and the rain
You can find your rainbow
Because you found it before
You did it

AUTHOR'S NOTE

Thank you dear reader for choosing to read Starlight Life. I wish you love, light, and luck on your own journey.

The idea of Starlight Life came to me from the belief that there is more to life than what we can see in front of our eyes. It came from a desire to write and explore spirituality, which eventually became this book. For I believe that we all have our own unique souls, and Starlight Life was created to inspire yours. May you fill the sky of your life with the shining stars of your wishes come true. May you also find magic in the little things. For it is in those moments that we learn to slow down, and appreciate our lives We are all learning and growing as human beings, and may we all love and care for our perfectly imperfect selves. I am still learning to do this, but I feel like we are all on our own unique journey of growth. I hope that this book has inspired you on your own path in some way. Many blessings to you.

ACKNOWLEDGEMENTS

This book would not be what it is if not for the love, support, and inspiration of some amazing people.

To my wonderful family. Thank you for loving me, supporting me and believing in me. I would not be the person I am today without you. I love you, and I am grateful to have you in my life. I wish you much love and happiness in your lives xxx

To my fantastic friends. Thank you for welcoming me into your lives, and being there for me. We have had many joyful times together, and I am grateful that you made me a part of them. I hope that we can have many more, because you mean a lot to me. xxx

To all of the great teachers who encouraged me, inspired me, and uplifted me. Not just in my education, but also through the difficult times I had at school. Thank you for all that you did for me, and for the education system. Many blessings to you xxx

To the brilliant illustrators at Gibble Pot. Thank you for working with me on this book, and thank you for your kindness and support. Your illustrations bring this book to life in a wonderful way. I hope that your lives are as beautiful as your illustrations xxx

To the terrific team at Book Baby. Thank you for answering any questions that I had in regards to publishing a book. Also, thank you for your patience and support. I wish you all the best xxx

To my incredible spiritual mentors. Thank you for your loving guidance, and for all the amazing work you do for the spiritual community. I have experienced many beautiful things that I would not have experienced without you. Love and light to you xxx

To my remarkable spirit guides. Thank you for your love, patience and tolerance. I know that a lot of the words within this book were inspired by you. I know that you are always there, even if I don't see you. I send you my love and gratitude. xxx

And last but not least to you, the reader. Thank you for being a part of this journey and reading Starlight Life. Thank you for following your heart. May it guide you to create a trail of love and light through this life, and beyond. For you are amazing, and you deserve to create a life of love and purpose today, tomorrow and beyond .Blessings, love and light to you xxx

ABOUT THE AUTHOR

N.C Brightman lives in Lancashire with her family and her pets. She has been writing since primary school, where she won a poetry competition. When she was in high school, she was diagnosed with Asperger's Syndrome. She believes that this is partly why she has been drawn to writing from a young age. She also feels that her perspective on life is helpful in the creative process. In her late teenage years, she became interested in spirituality, which started when she read her first copy of the magazine *Spirit and Destiny*. This is her first published book.

ABOUT THE ILLUSTRATORS

Gibble Pot are a husband and wife team with a personalised illustration business. They love creating bespoke gifts and stunning illustrations for special occasions, personal projects and loved ones. They illustrate by hand and paint with watercolours. Gibble Pot are based in Poulton le Fylde and deliver anywhere and everywhere.